Something To Think About

Robert H. Scott, Jr.

Something To Think About
ISBN: 979-8-218-00665-5

Copyright © 2022 Robert H. Scott, Jr.
Published by BayRob Publishing

"Something To Think About"

Meaning:

- To put something on your mind.
- To take into account.
- To consider. To ponder on.
- To think deeply about.
- To examine attentively.
- To think about carefully.
- To conceive, envision, imagine, and realize.
- To be spiritually aware of.

Contents

Foreword 1

    Doctor Demona Jackson-Warren 1

    Devere Duckett 3

Words From the Author 4

Looking Back Over My Life 5

A Strange New World 10

Food For Thought 13

How Well Do You Know Your Bible? 18

Understanding the Times 26

Common Questions People Ask 33

Who Is This Jesus We Talk About? 37

    Imagine Heaven 44

Broken Focus 65

Looking Through the Eyes Of God 52

Perilous Times 65

    Wars And Rumors of Wars 75

Securing Your Eternal Future 78

Dead Man Walking 85

Hell Is a Real Place 92

Sodom of Today 97

   Wickedness In the Earth 98

The Heart Of A Soldier 102

A Money Driven Society 104

About The Author 105

Foreword

Doctor Demona Jackson-Warren,

From the very first day that I met Robert Scott, at Grace Temple Christian Ministries, I knew that our lives were intertwined, and we had a lot in common. It has been my honor to have known him for over six years. We have both been blessed above and beyond our greatest expectations in the areas of music and ministry.

I think he may agree that one of our most cherished shared blessings as friends and colleagues is that we are co-hosts of the "Faithful Word Broadcast" on KCWGthetruth.com where we use our talents and gifts through music to reach out to others by teaching, preaching, and singing to inspire others to build a better relationship with God and to have the strength to overcome the struggles of life while striving to fulfill their purpose and destiny.

Robert Scott certainly serves as a wonderful example to me and all who come in contact with him. He is an anointed songwriter, singer, author, and minister who began his ministry at the age of 26 in Decatur, GA. His consistent love for God and His people is second to none. He lives what he sings and preaches about. He is both talented and gifted, born and chosen by God for such a time as this to reach the lost at any cost. For years, many have tuned in weekly to hear him on KCWGthetruth.com, a global Internet radio broadcast where he continues to inspire and uplift people all over the world.

In this book, something to think about, Robert Scott demonstrates his prolific writing abilities that will take you on a real-life journey. Robert Scott has compiled a litany of his messages over the years that gives us a peep into his life and the world as he sees it evolving today. This book is candid, compassionate, and cognizant, asking tough questions and addressing hard-hitting subject matters dealing with Heaven, Hell, health, money, and our body, mind, and spirit. This book is a must read!

Doctor Demona Jackson-Warren,
Co-pastor, Grace Temple Christian Ministries, Inc.
Riverdale, GA

Devere Duckett,

I have known Rob Scott for two thirds of my life. I would be remiss not to mention him as my brother. Robert Scott Jr. is one of the most determined people I've met in my life. He is a very determined young man who is always extremely professional. They say LeBron has drive in what he goes after. He hasn't met Robert Scott Jr. I've always told Rob that if he had $1,000,000, the world would be a better place because he can take nothing and turn it into something. I've seen what he can do with no budget and make things happen. He defines his life by his faith in God and has always been honorable, a true friend, and a brother. He is someone I'll cherish for the rest of my life. He's always been professional in all that he's done. I want you, the reader, to know that this is a very special man, on a mission for God. I give him my support. Although music is his first choice, he is sharing his story in the book is a part of his call to encourage people to live for Christ through whatever they may be going through.

Devere Duckett,
Singer, songwriter, producer and brother

Words From the Author

I'll never forget how my mission and assignment started out. On May 20th, 1984, at Green Pastures Christian Ministries in Decatur, GA, under the leadership of the late pastor Ron Gunby and now Apostle Collette Gunby, the Lord snatched me from Hell and brought me into the marvelous light.

From there I continued in ministry at Changing Lives for Christ Ministry in College Park, GA, under pastors Willie and Belinda Farmer. From there, God took me to the next level in ministry by starting The Faithful Word Broadcast on KCWGthetruth.com with a fellow brother, the Reverend Glenis Langlais.

I was once told by Apostle Collette Gunby (whom I consider my spiritual mother in the Lord), "When God's will becomes more important to you than anything else, He will work in you and accomplish things in your life that you never thought possible." I never forgot that, and it has come to pass. Stay tuned...

Robert H. Scott, Jr.

Looking Back Over My Life

I was born into this world before my time. I arrived two months premature. I came into the world early so I could get busy for God. It was at the age of 26 when I accepted Jesus Christ as my Lord and savior. Jeremiah 1:5 says, *"Before I formed thee in the belly I knew thee; and before thou camest forth out of the womb I sanctified thee, and I ordained thee a prophet unto the nations."* Jeremiah 29:11 says, *"For I know the thoughts that I think toward you, saith the Lord, thoughts of peace, and not of evil, to give you an expected end."*

Growing up in Atlanta, GA, I had two beautiful parents who were actually too young to be married. My dad drank a lot, which led to him not being the best he could have been in life. I vaguely remember some of the drunkenness I witnessed as a child. He'd get drunk, and the drama would start, which later led to a divorce.

My mother never remarried, but my father did. He and his new wife had one child, a girl. After that marriage ended in divorce, my dad fathered another child, a girl, by his live-in girlfriend in Compton, CA. Despite it all, my daddy was a good man. It amazes me how the brain works, how it stores stuff (memories). Growing up in southwest Atlanta brought about many challenges, but God had my back all along. When I was approximately 12 years old, I snuck into a swimming pool and almost drowned. But God! He had a plan for my life. That is why I'm still here. He has allowed me to be a blessing to others. He has given me platforms to witness to many people about the Gospel of Jesus Christ. He has given me revelation knowledge and allowed me to see things in the Heavens that blew me away.

At around age 13 or 14, I became very interested in music after watching Elvis Presley, The Temptations, The Chi-Lites, Blue Magic, and the Stylistics on television. I knew then that was what I wanted to do, and a recording artist was born. I formed my first singing group with some childhood friends, and we dominated the talent shows in the city. I knew I wanted to make records one day.

As I look back over my life, I'm amazed at how God has truly blessed me with an anointed gift to sing and write songs. He has allowed me to fulfill a lifelong dream of being a recording artist and working with the likes of Cameo, Curtis Mayfield, Georgia rappers, Raheem the Dream and Kilo Ali, and others. God has allowed me to actually hear my songs on the radio, and He has allowed me to sing on television numerous times. Looking back over my life, it's been bittersweet.

I have also been allowed to do some preproduction acting in two movies: The Staff (a faith-based movie), and a movie called New Black Wall Street. I have had new houses, cars, jewelry, nice clothes, and everything else that pertains to life and godliness. I've gone from being in debt to excellent credit, money in the bank, and, of course, loved ones who God allowed to truly bless me. I've done several music videos, and I am still counting.

Looking back over my life, I have been blessed to

travel to many, many places. I have my own gospel radio broadcast, a beautiful wife, and wonderful children. God has allowed me to see my children grow up, and now I see their children and their children's children. I never imagined myself writing a book, but God has blessed me with the opportunity to do so twice, and this book will be my third. I've had some good people in my life.

Looking back over my life, God has been good. I'm blessed to still be here, and I can truly say I'm proud to be a child of God. I know that His path leads to eternal life. One day I'll leave here and go to my eternal home (Heaven) where Jesus is. I have already prepared myself. What a blessing! I just want to reach as many people as I can before my departure. Today, if you will hear His voice, do not harden your heart (Hebrews 3:7).

God has allowed me to be a blessing to others. He has allowed me to witness to many about the Gospel of Jesus Christ. He has given me revelation knowledge and allowed me to see things in the Heavens which blew me away. He has given me platforms to reach people with the Gospel of Jesus Christ. I am blessed to still be here. Looking back over my life, I can truly say I am proud to be a child of God, giving my life to him. In the 1980s, before salvation, I was a part of one of the hottest bands on the Atlanta music scene, Pure Sugar.

As a young teenager, I left Atlanta to go to California to live with my dad. When I returned home to Atlanta, I went from the streets to the clubs, to the pulpit. It has been an amazing ride, and I've had some fun along the way. In the 1980s, before salvation, I was a part of Pure Sugar, one of the hottest bands on the Atlanta music scene. Once I came into the Ark, God had an assignment for me, but I had no idea what church was about until I got saved in 1984. I thank God for grace and mercy. I was at death's door one time, but God healed me. I have experimented with marijuana and cocaine, but I overcame all of that by the power of God by the age of twenty-six.

A Strange New World

In all my years, I've never seen a society as wicked as the one we are currently living in. Today, the love of many has waxed cold. Jesus told us that these times would come. The good, the bad, and the ugly. You would think the world (the unsaved) would run to the altar and repent when people started dying by the thousands, but many went right back to their same old way, with no repentance insight.

With all that has taken place, this should have been a wake-up call for all of us. Heartless criminals do anything and everything to get a dollar, even if it means taking a life. Many are so consumed with material things that they don't even acknowledge the importance of spiritual things. They are just marching through life without eternity in mind. The world is in a mess. We must be spiritually conscious as we get even closer to the coming of Christ. Jesus says for us to be ready because He's coming back at a time when we least expect it.

We're living in a time we've never seen before. The world is like a ball of confusion. As we witness the behaviors of others, it appears that many are losing their minds. Many have become wicked servants of Satan. According to Second Timothy 3:1, perilous times, or dangerous times, would come in the last days. We see it coming true every single day. The world has become like the days of Noah and the days of Sodom and Gomorrah. It's obvious that wickedness is in the atmosphere. Every year is more wicked than the year before and the decade before.

Noah tried to warn the people, but they refused to take heed, just like many are doing today because they love darkness rather than light. We're surrounded by pure darkness, and many don't want to come to the light. The behaviors and bad habits of many are on the rise.

The Word of God was written for our instruction.

- Luke 11:23 says, *"He who is not with Me is against Me, and he who does not gather with Me scatters."*

- The Apostle John said, *"Anyone whose father*

is God listens gladly to the Word of God. Since you don't, it proves you aren't God's children." (John 8:47).

- Jesus plainly said in Matthew Chapter 15, *"Many serve me with their lips and not with their hearts."* (see Matthew 15:8-9)

The devil influences multitudes into living for the moment, so when death comes, they are not ready. The time is urgent! Jesus is coming back. Give your life to Jesus Christ before it is too late. Do it in a hurry!

Food For Thought

Every one of us is on a path going somewhere. There are two roads that we travel on. One is wide, the other narrow. You determine your path as you travel through life's journey. Scripture says, *"Let every man work out his own salvation."* Church attendance without salvation will not get you into Heaven. You must be born again.

Have a talk with yourself and ask yourself this question: Am I prepared for eternal life, or will I wait until it's too late? Evaluate your life and your spiritual direction. Make your life count. Today (not tomorrow, not next week) is the day of salvation. I'm not here to debate the Word of God, but to give you the truth according to the Word of God. Get it while you can because, after death, there is no more opportunity to be saved.

In John 10:9, Jesus says, *"I am the door: by me if any man enter in, he shall be saved."* That is the only way you will be granted access into the city of God. It's only through Jesus Christ. My assignment as a minister of the gospel is to use the gifts and callings that God has put in me to point you to Jesus. There's no time to waste. The time is urgent!

My question to you, the reader, is how would you live your life if you knew you had only an hour left on earth? How sure are you that at the moment of death, God will welcome you into His presence? The Lord gives us gifts to use on the earth. The purpose of those gifts is for the perfecting of the Saints, (to equip us for service) for the work of the ministry. We must not sit on the gift, but rather stir it up.

"Neglect not the gift that is in you." — 1 Timothy 4:14

This refers to the call of God on your life and the anointing of the Holy Spirit upon the interview to carry out the call or task.

"Do the work of an evangelist. Make full proof of your ministry." — 2 Timothy 4:5

Keep trying to get people saved. Why? Life is short and uncertain, time is urgent.

"Therefore, my beloved brethren, be ye stedfast, unmoveable, always abounding in the work of the Lord, forasmuch as ye know that your labour is not in vain in the Lord." — *1 Corinthians 15:58*

To be steadfast means to be firmly fixed, not subject to change. The Lord wants us to open our mouths boldly to make known the mystery of the Gospel. We can't be afraid to tell others what the Lord says in His Word. It's up to them to accept it or reject it.

"But all who reject me, and my message will be judged on the day of judgment by the truth I have spoken." — *John 12:48 (ASV)*

It doesn't matter what anyone else says. Jesus said, and I quote, "I don't speak on my own authority. And I know His instructions lead to eternal life." (John 12:49) Make your life count. We must live with eternity in mind.

Question: Who will be at the Great White Throne of Judgement? Every unsaved person who has ever lived will be there at this judgement. God the Father has given Him (Jesus) authority to execute judgement. According to Revelation 20:12, there are two sets of books that are kept in Heaven: *"And I saw the dead, small and great, stand before God; and the books were opened: and another book was opened, which is the book of life: and the dead were judged out of those things which were written in the books, according to their works."*

One of these books contains the actions of every individual who has ever lived. The other book contains the names of all who gave themselves to Jesus, became a born-again Christian, and maintained their walk with him. We must realize everything is written down and yet for everyone who accepts Christ, all of the failures, sins, and transgressions are erased, are never to be remembered again.

The blood of Jesus has cleansed us from all sin (John 1:7). The word "cleansed" refers to a cleansing of our hearts and lives as well as being cleansed from the book. No unsaved person will have any excuse because everything they have ever done is registered, and they will not be able to deny it. Food for thought (spiritual food for your soul). I am a firm believer that spiritual food is needed to grow in the things of God. Matthew 4:4 says, *"It is written: 'Man shall not live on bread alone, but on every word that comes from the mouth of God.'"*

We are all in a race and our expectation is to win— to reach our target, Heaven. No one gets a prize for starting the race. The only person who gets a prize is the one who finishes the race. Hebrews 12:1 tells us to *"Run with patience the race that is set before us."* Keep running for your life. Many make a good start, but then fall by the wayside. We've got to get the Word of God on the inside of us to be able to stand strong against Satan. We are in a war against the forces of darkness.

How Well Do You Know Your Bible?

How well do you know this book of instructions (the Bible) given to us by God? Many people will challenge you on what you believe. Now, my question to you is can you prove what you believe? Is it biblical? Are you going to believe what you are taught or what God says? This is the problem with all these different beliefs, if it ain't written, it ain't real. 2nd Timothy 2:15 tells us, *"Study to shew thyself approved unto God, a workman that needeth not to be ashamed, rightly dividing the word of truth."*

1 John 4:1-5 says, *"Beloved, believe not every spirit, but try the spirits whether they are of God."* Why? *"Because many false prophets are gone out into the world. Hereby know ye the Spirit of God."* When you know your Bible, you can discern those who set forth false doctrine. People are saying all

kinds of things, and if it sounds good, many just accept it. We must determine if what they say lines up with what God says.

Remember, Satan's greatest weapon is deception. He always has a strategy in every attack. One of them is described in Ephesians 6:11 as a wile. A wile is a scheme that is hidden to deceive you. Every evil spirit has an assigned position or target, and one of Satan's targets is your mind. That is where the battlefield is. That is why we must be spiritually alert. We cannot be afraid to say what God says. 1st Thessalonians 5:21 talks about how we should examine everything carefully and hold fast to that which is good.

"Open your mouth boldly to make known the mystery of the gospel." — Ephesians 6:19

Then 1st Corinthians 2:14 tells us, *"But the natural man receiveth not the things of the Spirit of God* (speaking of the individual who is not born again) *for they are foolishness unto him* (lack of understanding) *neither can he know them, because they are spiritually discerned."*

Think about this, when Jesus walked the earth,

the religious leaders also tried to find fault in Him. They did not know their Bible (so to speak). Jesus told them, *"If you really knew God like you say you would know who I am."* All of us must realize who we are. To know about God and His Word can only be revealed to us by the Holy Spirit. Trying to understand God through natural means is impossible. Why? Because you are disconnected!

A lamp will not turn on unless it is plugged into the socket. The Bible tells us that God's Word is a lamp unto our feet and a light unto our path (Psalm 119:105). Without this lamp (light), the Word of God is dark to you, and you cannot see where you are going. In other words, you walk in darkness. The only lamp in the world that produces "true spiritual light" is the Bible. It is truly a road map for life, a blueprint for eternity. God's Word gives life, but you have got to want it. You've got to study it for yourself.

Since the Word of God is a road map for life, we must be cautious of following scriptural errors, as there are many false doctrines and biblical errors being taught to deceive and lead people astray. Jehovah's Witnesses, Mormons, Masons, and others are teaching false doctrine. I'm reminded of a conversation a member of the Jehovah's Witness and I had. We were discussing scripture, and he said that in Genesis 1:26, when God said, let us make man in our image, that God was talking to an angel. He was in error. Why? Because angels do not create.

God was with Jesus (the Word) and the Holy Spirit. All three are shown in this chapter, appearing together. The Father, the Son, and the Holy Spirit. Angels are messengers, not creators. Jesus was actually the flesh side of God. That's when God became man. He laid aside his expression of deity (deity means God supreme being) while never losing possession of His deity. Jesus is God, the Father is God, and the Holy Spirit is God. All three are called God in the Bible. (*Read the book of John*)

Throughout scripture God appears to be manifested in three. Jesus said, *"I came down from Heaven."* Jesus emptied himself of everything and became like man so that made him less than the Father.

Jesus gave up His glory (temporary) that he shared with the Father. When you give up something you are no longer equal. This was done until he went back to Heaven that's why Jesus prayed, *"Now, Father, bring me into the glory we shared before the world began"* (John 17:5).

> *"In the beginning was the Word, and the Word was with God, and the Word was God." — John 1:1*

The one known as Savior is Jesus Christ (Titus 3:4). It's a mystery and sometimes hard to understand. Again, understand this: When Jesus came down from Heaven through the virgin birth that was His entrance (in human form) into the earth realm. He stepped out of eternity into time. Before He came to the planet earth, He was in Heaven, in the eternal realm of God, outside of time. There He was known as the Word of God. Jesus was actually His earthly given name, given to him by the Father. In the book of Matthew 1:23, it says, *"Behold, the virgin shall be with child, and bear a Son, and they shall call His name Immanuel,"* which is translated, *"God with us."*

And the 25th chapter of Matthew describes how Mary gave birth to her firstborn son, and how his earthly father, Joseph, named him Jesus, which means Savior. Christ is the visible image of the invisible God. He was actually God with skin on. The flesh side of God. He existed before anything was created and reigns supreme over all creation, as God created everything in the heavenly realms and on Earth through Him. He made the things we can see, and the things we can't see, such as thrones, kingdoms, rulers, and authorities in the unseen world. Everything was created through Him and for Him. He existed before anything else, and he holds all creation together.

In John the 8th chapter, Jesus said, *"He who follows me shall not walk in darkness but shall have the light of life."* So, if you're not following Jesus, you walk in darkness. He also said in John 18:37, "everyone who is of the truth hears my voice." There are many voices out there. Who are you listening to?

"Whosoever transgresseth, and abideth not in the doctrine (teaching) of Christ, hath not God. He that abideth in the doctrine of Christ, he hath both the Father and the Son." — *John 9:11 (KJV)*

You don't even have God if you're not teaching Christ. You must be born again. It's a spiritual birth. Remember, man has already had a natural birth. But now man must have a spiritual birth. Without it, man cannot comprehend or understand God's way of doing things. We must be very careful about what we get involved in because we may be opening the door to satanic oppression. I watched a popular TV show where the host had a guest on who was a spirit medium. This person was supposedly contacting people's deceased loved ones. All of this is totally satanic (necromancy). Anyone who practices this is totally dealing with demon spirits. (*See Leviticus 20:6, 20:27*) As I was watching this show, I was saying to myself how foolish these people actually thought they were communicating with the dead and receiving messages from them.

> *"¹ Now the Spirit speaketh expressly, that in the latter times some shall depart from the faith, giving heed to seducing spirits, and doctrines of devils; ² Speaking lies in hypocrisy; having their conscience seared with a hot iron." — 1 Timothy 4:1-2 (KJV)*

The Bible says the Word was made flesh and dwelt among us. Jesus lived among us. He walked on the earth. He is real. God came down from Heaven and lived among us in the flesh. What we do with the Bible will affect where we will spend eternity. We must be about God's agenda. We cannot give all our attention to everything else. We have to spend more time in His Word. We must know our Bible.

The Holy Spirit inspired men to speak from God. (2 Samuel 23:2, 2 Peter 1:19) The Bible is a book of history, prophecy, promises, and instructions. It's our instruction manual on how to live this earthly life and prepare for Heaven and how to avoid Hell.

Understanding the Times

According to 2nd Timothy 3:1, we're living in perilous times, dangerous times. Nowadays, you can't live your life without looking over your shoulders. Never before has it been more evident that we're living in the last of the last days. Many in today's society are desperate and reckless. Sin is rampant on earth. As we get closer to the final confrontation between God and Satan (good and evil), trouble is all around us.

It appears that there is no end in sight to all the madness that's taking place on earth. As we watch television and hear the weatherman talk about the worst hurricanes in history sweeping across the land with mass destruction, many lose their homes and their lives. From city to city, state to state, country to country, evil and destruction are everywhere.

Things sometimes happen suddenly. With all the

violence, floods, storms, earthquakes, etc. that are happening in the world, the rapture can't be that far off. Satan's goal is to keep many in ignorance of what's really going on. We're on the front line of a real spiritual war, so the Bible tells us to be sober, alert, and vigilant and ready at all times because our adversary, the devil, walks about like a roaring lion, seeking whom he may devour. Yet I see a great falling away of church members. Many are falling back into their old ways.

Children are not taught that they are sinners and in need of a Savior, and so many grow up to be ticking time bombs, lacking any morals at all, committing unthinkable crimes. They are out of control. As we all watch what is taking place in the world today, in your city and mine, the insane things people do today are on the rise. Jesus is coming. There are two great powers at war in our thought life, and each strives to change our lives. While Satan appeals to our flesh, the Holy Spirit encourages us to get closer to God.

Satan works 24 hours a day to wreck and ruin people's lives, killing many by the thousands. He comes to steal, kill, and destroy, and your mind is the target. Mental illness is on the rise. It seems like people have lost their minds, and, of course, there are those who are simply just stuck on stupid. People have become so cruel and cold-hearted, disrespectful, and unholy.

There used to be respect for the House of God, but not anymore. Some preachers now have to carry a gun on them in the pulpit. Satan is the prince of the power of the air. Ephesians 2:2 says he operates in the spirit realm. Today's society looks different from 30 years ago. Television is different. Anything and everything takes place on social media today. It is like we're living in a modern-day Sodom and Gomorrah, with no signs of things getting better.

> *"24 Wherefore God also gave them up to uncleanness through the lusts of their own hearts, to dishonour their own bodies between themselves (every type of immorality): 25 who changed the truth of God into a lie, and worshipped and served the creature more than the Creator, who is blessed for ever. Amen. 26 For this cause God gave them up unto vile affections: for even their*

women did change the natural use into that which is against nature: *27 And likewise also the men, leaving the natural use of the woman, burned in their lust one toward another (homosexuals); men with men working that which is unseemly, and receiving in themselves that recompence of their error which was meet. 28 And even as they did not like to retain God in their knowledge, God gave them over to a reprobate mind, to do those things which are not convenient."* — *Romans 1:24-28*

God made two genders. Mark 10:6 says, *"But from the beginning of the creation, God made them male and female."* Male and female, not male and female and something else. In Genesis 5:2 it says, *"Male and female created he them; and blessed them, and called their name Adam, in the day when they were created."* Anything other than that is from Satan. Transgender is a creation of Satan, not God.

God instituted marriage and ordained it to be between two classes of people: a man and a woman, male and female, not two females, not two males. It is an abomination. God said so! The dictionary defines "abomination" as a thing that causes disgust or hatred, a vile, shameful, or detestable action, condition, or habit. No preacher or court can change the rules. God alone designed marriage, not our former president. God has nothing to do with same-sex marriage. It is a counterfeit. It's not real.

So, same-sex marriages are not valid in God's eyes. Why, because it goes against God's laws. Not valid, meaning being without foundation or force, truth, unfounded, groundless, unwarranted, unjustified, legally void, not binding, improper, illegal, and null and void. It is sickening to see a man on television kissing another man or two women kissing each other as a man and a woman would do openly on television, and to watch men talking about their husbands and women talking about this is my wife. God is not pleased.

I may get some backlash for saying this, but I say what God says. It doesn't matter to me what anyone else thinks. I'm concerned about what God thinks of me. It's about us understanding the times we are living in. There are two destinations, Heaven, and Hell.

There are two ways man will live, the right way and the wrong way. There are two roads we travel on. One is narrow, the other is wide. Most people are on the wide road that leads to destruction. The narrow road leads to life.

Philippians 2:12 tells us to *"work out your own salvation with fear and trembling."* Either you are saved, or you are lost. Many are marching through life like there is no God, like there is no eternity. We're living in a world that's unpredictable and dark, and the answer is Jesus Christ, not the White House, not somebody else's house. Everyone in the White House appears to be confused, but the one who sits on the throne has the answer to everything. These are the times we're living in.

Man has free will to choose between these two warring spirits. Jesus said, just as it was in Noah's time, so it will be in ours. So, I'm saying today, get into the Ark while there is still time. The COVID-19 coronavirus that has killed hundreds of thousands of people should have had many running to the altar, running to God. Today's Ark is Jesus Christ. The same cry that Noah had is in the air in our lifetime throughout the Gospel of Jesus Christ.

"In all your ways acknowledge Him, And He shall direct your paths." — Proverbs 3:6

The Word of God tells us to be anxious for nothing but in everything by prayer and petition with Thanksgiving present your requests to God (Philippians 4:6). James 1:5 says, *"if any of you lacks wisdom, he should ask God who gives generously to all without finding fault and it will be given to him."* Many of the so-called experts lack wisdom in dealing with all the darkness going on in the world. Our direction in dealing with the world's problems comes from above.

Common Questions People Ask

There are common questions people ask when someone gives you a personal prophecy.

Q: Do you run with it with what they said, or do you evaluate it?

A: Personal prophecy should be confirmation of what God has already told you most of the time.

Q: Does water baptism save you?

A: I would say it plays a part, but it alone doesn't save you. I believe confession is made unto salvation and it works in combination with water baptism which is an outward show of your transformation into the family of God, but water baptism alone does not save you.

Q: Can you get to Heaven without being a Christian or being saved?

A: I say no unless you are a baby or under the age of accountability. You cannot get to Heaven by any other means than through Jesus Christ. If you confess Jesus Christ as Lord and Savior and repent of your sin and ask him to come into your heart, you are saved. A spiritual transformation must take place, going from the natural man to the spiritual man. (See John 3:16, John 10:1)

Q: Why are there so many religions? which is which one is right?

A: We must understand that there are many religions but only one truth. Jesus said it himself when he said in John 10:9 *"I am the door. If anyone enters by Me, he will be saved, and will go in and out and find pasture."*

In John 14:6 *"I am the way and the truth and the life. No one comes to the Father except through me."* (NIV)

Acts 4:12 says, *"Neither is there salvation in any other: for there is none other name under Heaven given among men, whereby we must be saved."* (KJV)

Q: Who will walk in the city of gold, the new Jerusalem?

A: John said, *"the nations of them which are saved shall walk in the light of it."* (Revelation 21:24)

We are also told Revelation 21:27 *"But there shall by no means enter it anything that defiles, or causes an abomination or a lie, but only those who are written in the Lamb's Book of Life."* (NKJV)

Revelation 22:14 says, *"Blessed are those who do His commandments, that they may have the right to the tree of life, and may enter through the gates into the city." so as you can see not just anyone will be able to enter and only those whose name is written in the lambs book of life is*

Q: Is it possible for an unsaved person to believe that they are saved just because they go to church?

A: I think it is possible. Many people live a worldly lifestyle and go to church on Sunday, believing they are saved and going to Heaven, but they may never have accepted Jesus Christ as Lord and Savior. They just go to church. Proverbs 14:12 warns that there is a way which seems right to a man, but its end is the way of death.

> *"Be sober, be vigilant; because your adversary the devil, as a roaring lion, walketh about, seeking whom he may devour."* — *1 Peter 5:8*

We live in a satanic world that's being ruled from high places. The deadliest enemy is the one you can't see. Many today would rather fill up a football stadium to watch a game than fill up a church to save their soul. *Uhm...Something to think about.*

> *"Am I therefore become your enemy, because I tell you the truth?"* — *Galatians 4:16*

Don't get mad when someone tells you about God. They are only trying to warn you about the reality that will one day come true. Jesus came to seek and save the last.

Who Is This Jesus We Talk About?

Let's talk about the mystery of who He really is according to the word of God. Where did Jesus come from?

"For I have come down from Heaven, not to do My own will, but the will of Him who sent Me." — *John 6:38*

Jesus stepped out of eternity into time. Jesus was God with skin on.

"You search the Scriptures, for in them you think you have eternal life; and these are they which testify of Me." — *John 5:39*

Jesus told us that the Scriptures point to Him. During his earthly journey, despite the fact of who Christ was and what he did, only a few accepted him as the Messiah. The same is true today. He is who He says he is. Jesus is identified as the Word.

"¹ In the beginning was the Word, and the Word

was with God, and the Word was God. 3 All things were made by him; and without him was not any thing made that was made." — John 1:1,3 (KJV)

"Behold, a virgin shall be with child, and shall bring forth a son, and they shall call his name Emmanuel, which being interpreted is, God with us." — Matthew 1:23 (KJV)

Remember in John 10:30 Jesus' disciple Thomas addressed Jesus as my Lord and my God.

Isaiah 9:6 *"For unto us a Child is born,"* (which we saw happen according to scripture through the Virgin Mary) *"Unto us a Son is given; And the government will be upon His shoulder. And His name will be called Wonderful, Counselor, Mighty God, Everlasting Father, Prince of Peace."* Actually, when Jesus came down from Heaven to planet earth through Mary, that was His entrance into the earth realm, He was the flesh side of God.

That's why the Word says that He was God manifested or revealed in the flesh. As you read in John 12:44, God became man temporarily. It says Jesus shouted to the crowd, *"He who believes in Me, believes not in Me but in Him who sent Me."* In other words, if you trust Jesus, you are really trusting God. In John 5:9, He goes on to say that the scriptures point to Him. I believe when you see Jesus, you are seeing God manifested in the person of Jesus Christ. As I study the Word of God, it all makes sense.

Again, I'm talking about who this Jesus is we all talk about. Philippians 2:5 says your attitude should be the kind that was shown to us by Jesus Christ, who, though he was God, did not demand and cling (hold onto) to His right as God, but laid aside His mighty power and glory, taking the disguise of a slave or serv-ant, becoming like man. In other words, He came to earth, completed his assignment after 33 years, and returned to where He came from — back to Heaven. In John 12:23-24, Jesus said that the time had come for him to return to His glory in Heaven.

"And now, O Father, glorify Me together with Yourself, with the glory which I had with You be-fore the world was." — John 17:5

Remember when He left Heaven and came to earth, He laid His power and glory aside temporarily. That's why He said the Father is greater than I (John 14:28). He said that because of the state He was in as a man. At that time, He became a servant. Remember, the servant is not greater than his Lord.

> *"Don't ever forget the wonderful fact that Jesus Christ was a man, born into King David's family; and that he was God, as shown by the fact that he rose again from the dead."* — *2 Timothy 2:8 (TLB)*

> *"Let all the angels of God worship Him* (Jesus)*."* — *Hebrews 1:6*

> *"Your kingdom, O God, will last forever and ever; its commands are always just and right. You love right and hate wrong; so God, even your God, has poured out more gladness upon you than on anyone else."* — *Hebrews 1:8-9*

Remember, in Heaven they share glory. Genesis 1:26 says, *"Let us make man like one in our image after our likeness."* This sounds more like one. In Acts 3:22, Moses said *"The Lord God will raise up a Prophet among you, who will resemble me! Listen carefully to everything he tells you."*

In Isaiah 43:10 God the Son, speaking to the nation of Israel says:

"You are My witnesses," says the Lord, "And My

servant whom I have chosen, that you may know and believe Me, and understand that I am He. Before Me there was no God formed (or revealed), *nor shall there be after Me.*

So, the only God formed was Jesus Christ. He was manifested in the flesh. We see God through Jesus Christ.

In Isaiah 44:24, God the Son, speaking, says:

The Lord, your Redeemer who made you, says: All things were made by me; I alone stretched out the Heavens. By myself I made the earth and everything in it. I am the one who shows what liars all false prophets are, by causing something else to happen than the things they say. I make wise men give opposite advice to what they should and make them into fools." (Living Bible)

In Isaiah 45:21-24, God the Son, speaking through the prophet Isaiah, says:

"21 Who declared it of old? Was it not I, the Lord? And there is no other god besides me, a righteous God and a Savior; there is none besides me.

Here He's calling himself God and Savior:

"22 Look to Me, and be saved, all you ends of the earth! For I am God, and there is no other. 23 I have sworn by Myself; the word has gone out of My mouth in righteousness, and shall not return, that to Me every knee shall bow, every tongue shall take an oath. 24 He shall say, 'surely in the Lord I have righteousness and strength. To Him men shall come, and all shall be ashamed who are incensed against Him."

"Let the word of Christ dwell in you richly in all wisdom; teaching and admonishing one another in psalms and hymns and spiritual songs, singing with grace in your hearts to the Lord." — Colossians 3:16 (KJV)

Let the words of Christ and how their richness live (or dwell) in your hearts and make you wise.

"Christ is the visible image of the invisible God. He existed before anything was created and is supreme over all creation." — Colossians 1:15 (NLT)

Christ is the exact likeness of the unseen God and existed before God made anything at all. Exact likeness means having the same features, acting in the same ways, and so on.

"I am the Lord, and there is no one else; there is no God except Me."— Isaiah 45:5

It's like this: if you take an egg, it has three parts, but yet it is one egg: the shell, the white part, and the yolk. I believe each person of the godhead had an assignment. The Bible teaches that there is only one God, yet all three—Father, Son, and Holy Spirit, are called God in scripture. It's hard to understand sometimes, but God's Word doesn't lie.

"He that honoureth not the Son honoureth not the Father which hath sent him."— John 5:23 (KJV)

You cannot honor one without the other. Again, Jesus said no man comes to the Father except through me.

"Who, being in the form of God, thought it not robbery to be equal with God."— Philippians 2:6

Jesus being in the form of God thought it was not robbery to be equal with God.

"Jesus shouted to the crowds, "If you trust me, you are really trusting God."— John 12:44 (LB)

Jesus was speaking to Thomas one day and said, "You see, Thomas, no one can get to the father except by means of me. I am flesh, the spirit is on the inside. Thomas if you had known who I am then you would have known who my Father is, so from now on, you know Him and have seen Him. Who? The Father because I am in the Father and the Father is in me. Phillip says, *"Sir, show us the Father, and we will be satisfied."* Jesus replied, *"Don't you yet know who I am. I am the Father manifested in the flesh in the person of Jesus Christ."* (see John 14)

"Whoever transgresses and does not abide in the doctrine of Christ does not have God. He who abides in the doctrine of Christ has both the Father and the Son." — 2 John 1:9 (NKJV)

Someone said to me that Jesus never existed. He was made up by the Europeans. So, who is this Jesus we've been talking about? He is God. In the end, this person and everyone who rejects Jesus will know that Jesus is God. Every knee will bow and confess that Jesus Christ is Lord.

Imagine Heaven

Our imagination takes us many places. The book

of Revelation tells us about a place called Heaven, where all believers in Christ will go one day when their life on earth has expired. How would your life change if you knew the exact year and day that you would die? We must remember that all of us have an appointment with death.

Heaven is a place that is so beautiful beyond our imagination, and the Lord has given us a little sneak peek of what it looks like in the book of Revelation, the 21st chapter, when John talks about how he was carried away in the spirit to a great and high mountain and shouted and showed him this great city, the Holy Jerusalem.

Your ticket to Heaven doesn't cost you anything because Jesus has already paid for it. Listen! The way to Heaven is restricted to just one avenue, through Jesus Christ. Many, and I say many, will seek to find an alternative route to Heaven with God, but there is none. Jesus has already told us there's only one way, and He is it. There aren't many doors. How many ways to Heaven ain't no side door, ain't no back door? Jesus is the door.

Stay in the race toward Heaven; watch and pray;

be alert! Why? Because Satan's job is to keep you from finishing the race toward Heaven. He wants to disqualify you with distractions and all kinds of works of the flesh. Jesus wants us to run from the very appearance of evil. The new Jerusalem will be a city that will be breathtaking. God said there will be a new Heaven and a new earth with Heaven descending out of Heaven to planet earth where we will live eternally with God.

> *"10 And he carried me away in the spirit to a great and high mountain, and shewed me that great city, the holy Jerusalem, descending out of Heaven from God, 11 Having the glory of God: and her light was like unto a stone most precious, even like a jasper stone, clear as crystal; 12 And had a wall great and high, and had twelve gates, and at the gates twelve angels, and names written thereon, which are the names of the twelve tribes of the children of Israel." — Revelation 21:10-12*

Question: Is your name written in the Lamb's Book of Life? It's the roster in Heaven with the names of every believer. Remember, in order to get to this place called Heaven, you have to either die or miss death by going up in the rapture. Several people have said they visited Heaven in a dream or vision and have said how beautiful it is. Otherwise, we just have to imagine Heaven from what God has told us in His word until we get there. What a glorious day that will be! There are conditions you must first meet in order to get there. You must be born again and walk in the light as He (Jesus) is in the light (walk in His ways).

The Word of God tells us in Revelation 21:24 that *"the nations of those who are saved shall walk in its light."* So, to get to Heaven you must be saved, as Jesus promises in the Gospel of John when He said in John 14:1-3 says:

"¹ Let not your heart be troubled; you believe in God, believe also in Me. ² In My Father's house are many mansions; if it were not so, (I don't lie) I would have told you. I go to prepare a place for you. ³ And if I go and prepare a place for you, I will come again and receive you to Myself; that where I am, there you may be also." (NKJV)

If you ask most people if they think they will go to Heaven when they die, most will say yes! Some will say I hope so, or I think so, but today, before your life expires on earth, you can be sure, especially if you haven't already done so. We must remember that Heaven is a real place. It's the dwelling place of God, where Jesus sits at the right hand of God. He will be there. His throne is there. The angels are there. There are many people there who once lived here on earth. While we are living on earth, we should be working on getting our house (hearts) in order and preparing for the coming of the Lord.

Philippians 3:20 says our citizenship is in Heaven. Heaven is designed and built by God. Hebrews 11:10 says, *"For he looked for a city which hath foundations, whose builder and maker is God."* God has made it possible for all of us to go to Heaven. Jesus laid down his life, making the path possible. Unfortunately, many will not make it.

When you reject Jesus Christ as Lord and Savior, you reject all hope beyond the grave. Jesus has plainly said in John 14:6 *"I am the way, the truth, and the life. No one comes to the Father except through Me."* In John 10:9, He says, *"I am the door. If anyone enters by me, he will be saved."* Admission is needed to enter, and Jesus is the admission ticket. Nobody passes without going through the door, and nobody is sneaking in. If you don't get in through Jesus Christ (God manifested in the flesh), you won't be able to access it. Access will be denied. Heaven is God's prepared place for a prepared people. To be prepared, you prepare ahead of time.

For all of those who are born-again Christians, you have hope beyond the grave. God said in 1 Corinthians 2:9, *"Eye has not seen, nor ear heard, neither have entered into the heart of man, the things which God has prepared for them that love him."* We, as born-again believers, must continue to keep pressing our way through. It's easy sometimes to get distracted in life, but we have got to keep going. We have got to be determined in our hearts to make it to Heaven when God calls us by our name and says "enter in." I want to hear those words, "well done, my good and faithful servant."

Many don't even think about Heaven or avoiding Hell until it's too late. Think about this: there is an expiration date on our earthly life, but in Heaven, where we will be forever with Jesus, it will be timeless. One day, this journey will be over. It will come to an end. Then which way are you going? You decide.

John 3:3 — "Except a man be born again, he cannot see the kingdom of God."

Imagine Heaven. We must stay focused on the road to Heaven. Things may get a little bumpy along the way, or you may veer off onto the wrong road, but don't give up. Repent and get back on the straight and narrow. It will be all worth it in the end.

None of us knows the day or hour of our departure when our spirit and soul will exit this earth, leaving our bodies behind, going from earth to Heaven, from this location to another location. That's that blessed hope that I look forward to. While I'm still on earth, I want to help others get their Heavenly citizenship. That's why we must be about the Father's business. If you have not prepared for Heaven, you are already prepared for Hell.

Hebrews 11:25-27 says that Moses habitually looked away from the treasures in Egypt and purposely fixed his eyes on the Heavenly reward. Moses understood that the pressures and treasures of this world last only for a moment. Nicodemus, in his natural state of mind, said to Jesus, "How can a man be born again when he is old?"

Nicodemus had no knowledge of what Jesus was saying. If he had been truly born again, he would have understood these terms. Nicodemus went on to say, can he enter a second time into his mother's womb and be born again? Jesus answered and said, "Verily, verily, except a man be born of water and of the Spirit, he cannot enter into the kingdom of God."

"But we speak the wisdom of God in a mystery, even the hidden wisdom, which God ordained before the world unto our glory." — 1 Corinthians 2:7

The hidden has to be revealed to you by God. You cannot figure it out. It's spiritually discerned. As a spiritual leader, Nicodemus should have known the way of salvation, but he didn't. We have got to be on a soul winning mission, so others can get to Heaven.

Looking Through the Eyes Of God

God is all knowing, and He is omnipresent. He sees the good, the bad, and the ugly. This means we must see others as God sees them and see ourselves through his eyes. When looking at others, do you see those who need a savior? We see through the eyes of God through His Word.

"I have chosen the way of truth; Your judgments I have laid before me." — Psalm 119:30

"Forever, O Lord, Your word is settled in Heaven." — Psalm 119:89

Looking through the eyes of God, I see a nation that has forgotten God, and many won't even acknowledge the Lord Jesus Christ. Many will say God, but most won't mention Jesus, or they will say the Most High. But He has a name that is above every name. We've all experienced, at one time or another, the pep talks given to us by an uncle or aunt, a grand-dad or grandma, etc. A "pep talk" is a short speech that is given to encourage someone to work harder to feel confident. Some of us got something out of it, and some dismissed it altogether, and as a result, we go through the pitfalls we could have avoided. Looking through the eyes of God (our Father), I have learned about all the things He tries to teach us; things to avoid and how to live, etc.

People ruin their lives through their own foolishness and then get angry at the Lord (Proverbs 19:3). Sometimes we need to have a talk with ourselves before we do anything foolish. Think before you act! As I sit and watch the evening news, I see the crimes being committed among our young people, and it's very foolish and disturbing behavior. The voice of the enemy is leading many astray and ruining their lives through criminal activities (robbery, murder, etc.). It's like we're dealing with a generation of fools without any hope. But there is hope. If they would only take heed. Jesus Christ is the answer.

Violence and strife appear in every city and state

across America. Many think they are going to get away with it, until the cops come knocking on their door! Or they see their ugly faces on the news. If you want money, go to work, get a job, and if you're just too lazy to work, that's when the enemy starts giving you ideas on how to rob someone. When the perpetrator gets caught, that's the very beginning of you creating a paper trail that will follow you for the rest of your life. From juvenile to jail, from jail to prison, these criminal offenses will catch up with you and the end result, if you don't change, can sometimes land you in the cemetery.

Why do I say that? Because many have lost their lives in the commission of a crime, and many have lost their lives in the streets. It's all about avoiding Hell before you expire on this earth. It's either grow up and do the right thing according to the Word of God or do it your way and miss Heaven. We're living in a world where you will have to make a choice about whom you're going to serve. Satan wants your soul. He wants to destroy your life. That's why he puts crazy criminal thoughts in your mind.

Too many people are falling victim to the streets, to the drug trade, and to all sorts of crimes in general. It's a trap! Satan will rob you of your freedom and then your soul. Now ask yourself if it's really worth it to be separated from your family and friends, to be locked up in a cell for the majority of the day every day for years, and to have to fight for your food and your manhood at times against those inmates who have no love for anyone except themselves and you seeing others get taken or stabbed. Is it worth it...? No!

When the judge says life without parole whatcha gonna do? Young man, young woman think! Think! Think! You don't have a clue of the reality that you're about to step into until it's too late. There's no easy way out eventually you're going to get caught get out of the danger zone! Don't hang around those who are always up to no good. Many are in the dungeons of prison life because of a bad choice because they wouldn't listen to God or to those who gave them good sound advice warning them of the pitfalls.

"Wherefore he saith, awake thou that sleepest, and arise from the dead, and Christ shall give thee light." — Ephesians 5:14

Arise from the dead to the things of the Spirit and Christ shall give you light. We have to take our life and our time on earth seriously before our time expires. All of us have been granted 24 hours in a day and it's up to us to use it wisely.

Ephesians 5:16-17 says, *redeeming the time, because the days are evil. Therefore do not be unwise, but understand what the will of the Lord is.* Time is precious because God has given us only a few short days to make choices that will bring eternal consequences don't destroy your life before it can get started you could have a good life and a brighter future if you would only heed God's Word.

"My son, give me your heart, and let your eyes observe my ways." — Proverbs 23:26

When I was a teenager, I did some foolish things, but I turned things around. Satan is always lurking around, seeking whom he may devour. He puts thoughts, suggestions, and ideas in your head to do evil, to kill, steal, and destroy. We all must be watchful and alert, so the wolf won't catch us off guard. We all must discern who's talking to us. Many young and old start to believe all the poison they see in movies, video games, and rap videos, and they try to act out what they see in real life.

> *"Don't do as the wicked do, and don't follow the path of evildoers." — Proverbs 4:14 NLT*

> *"Look straight ahead, and fix your eyes on what lies before you." — Proverbs 4:25*

When I was working as a law enforcement officer, there were teenagers being booked into jail for armed robbery, murder, etc. Some were young and not even out of school yet, with milk still on their breath. They were so young, but they chose the wrong path, and in the process, they began chapters in their lives that would ruin their future forever unless they made a U-turn off of that wide road they had started on. Many don't even realize we need God's GPS (**G**od's **P**lan of **S**alvation) to lead us the right way.

> *"A prudent person foresees danger and takes precautions. The simpleton (foolish or gullible) goes blindly on and suffers the consequences." — Proverbs 27:12*

I've always been that person who would listen to

good sound advice that would carry me through life and make me a better man.

"My son, attend to my words; incline thine ear unto my sayings. Let them not depart from thine eyes; keep them in the midst of thine heart." — Proverbs 4:20

I'm a witness that heeding good advice is true. I'm a product of what was said to me. It works! My granddaddy, Daniel M. Scott, Sr., said to me on many occasions, "Robert, seek ye first the Kingdom of God and all of his righteousness" (God's way of doing things). My spiritual mom and dad in the Lord would always tell me the do's and don'ts as I traveled this road. They would always encourage me and plant seeds of love and the Word of God in me.

Many don't want to listen to those who have already traveled down that road, and they are trying to keep you from making those same mistakes. I was always encouraged to finish school by my granddaddy. My mother, Barbara, my granddaddy, and my wife were truly very supportive of my music and my spiritual mom and dad, Gloria and Charles, were very supportive of me.

> *"Everyone admires a man of principles, but the one with a corrupt heart is despised." — Proverbs 12:8 TPT*

> *"Fools think their own way is right, but the wise listen to others." — Proverbs 12:15 NLT*

So, if you go through life thinking you know everything and have all the answers, you're a fool. I keep on going in my quest to make positive music that will reach hearts and touch lives. I keep on going because I can't quit. I'm determined to keep using my God gifted talents until my last breath. Especially when I have platinum and gold recording artists like my brother and my friend, the legendary Ted Wizard Mills, the original lead singer and the voice behind the R&B group Blue Magic, who inspires me and always gives me good sound advice.

Also, my little brother Devere, a worldwide recording artist and songwriter producer who has sung with the likes of The Temptations, KC and JoJo, Jasmine Guy, Bobby Brown, After 7, Stevie Wonder, The Dog Pound, Ice Cube, etc., etc., etc., and the list goes on and on. Currently, he's performing and touring with The Al McKay All Stars, in which Al McKay is an original member of Earth, Wind, And Fire. Also, people like Larry Billinger, Nesptah Soitis, So It Is, Carl Newson, Raimundo Thomas, Kevin B. Hunter, Sr., and the list of names are too long to mention. I thank God for allowing me to share my gift of song with the world.

In Deuteronomy 30:19 Moses said, "*I call Heaven and earth as witnesses today against you, that I have set before you life and death, blessing and cursing; therefore choose life, that both you and your descendants may live.*" remember Heaven is recording everything we do from the time of a child until our last breath that's why we must make our life count.

"Corrupt people walk a thorny, treacherous road; whoever values life will avoid it." — Proverbs 22:5

"The highway of the upright is to depart from evil: he that keepeth his way preserveth his soul." — Proverbs 16:17

"We can make our plans, but the Lord determines

our steps." — Proverbs 16:9

"People who accept discipline are on the pathway to life, but those who ignore correction will go astray." — Proverbs 10:17

Some people catch a case by being in the wrong company of friends or being in the wrong place at the wrong time choose your friends wisely bad company corrupts good character if you have a goal or a dream in life to succeed in something don't start doing stupid things because your dreams could be shattered by making wrong choices you can be young and foolish you can also be old and foolish think before you act Ecclesiastes 10:1 says, *"dead flies will cause even a bottle of perfume to stink!"* Yes, an ounce of foolishness can outweigh a pound of wisdom and honor.

"Don't let the excitement of youth cause you to forget your Creator. Honor him in your youth before you grow old and say, "Life is not pleasant anymore." — Ecclesiastes 12:1

The fear of the Lord is the beginning of knowledge: but fools despise wisdom and instruction." — Proverbs 1:7

"A wise person is hungry for knowledge, while the

fool feeds on trash." — Proverbs 15:14 NLT

"10 If young toughs tell you, "Come and join us"— turn your back on them! 11 "We'll hide and rob and kill," they say. 12 "Good or bad, we'll treat them all alike. 13 And the loot we'll get! All kinds of stuff! 14 Come on, throw in your lot with us; we'll split with you in equal shares." 15 Don't do it, son! Stay far from men like that, 16 for crime is their way of life, and murder is their specialty.

17 When a bird sees a trap being set, it stays away, 18 but not these men; they trap themselves! They lay a booby trap for their own lives. 19 Such is the fate of all who live by violence and murder. They will die a violent death." — Proverbs 1:10-19 Living Bible

"29 For you closed your eyes to the facts and did not choose to reverence and trust the Lord, 30 and you turned your back on me, spurning my advice. — Proverbs 1:29

Young people who obey the law are wise; those with wild friends bring shame to their parents. — Proverbs 28:7

I believe sometimes a lot of young people go out

and search for love and commit crimes of passion because they don't feel loved, or peer pressure gets the best of them by trying to fit in with what's popular, and as a result, it can backfire and lead you down the wrong path. The Bible plainly says, *"If you love sleep, you will end up in poverty. Stay awake, work hard; there will be plenty to eat."* (Proverbs 20:13 NLT).

"A wise youth harvests in the summer, but one who sleeps during harvest is a disgrace." — *Proverbs 10:5 NLT*

Romans 12:2 in the New Living Translation says, *"Don't copy the behavior and customs of this world, but let God transform you into a new person by changing the way you think. Then you will learn to know God's will for you, which is good and pleasing and perfect."* I'm looking at you through the eyes of God. God's way is the right way. God's instructions are in the Bible.

It's a choice for all of us to become the salt of the earth, a light in the dark places, and the only way that can happen is if we live for God, avoid the traps, and be determined to worship Him. I heard a minister say it like this: when salt loses its savor, it is useless. That is why we must make our life count. Do the work of an evangelist. Only what we do for Christ will last. Everything else will fade away.

Broken Focus

It is so important to stay focused and be watchful and alert. Some people's focus has been shattered by church hurt, and many have left the church because of it. Nothing is worth losing your salvation over. Being focused is so important because your soul is at stake.

"Set your mind on things above, not on things on the earth." — Colossians 3:2 (NKJV)

"But seek first the kingdom of God and His righteousness, and all these things shall be added to you." — Matthew 6:33 (NKJV)

My granddad used to always tell me that time keeps on moving. One day, our time will be up. Then what? We must keep our eyes on the prize. We must because we have a race to finish. We cannot let people break our focus and cause us to be disqualified in our race toward Heaven. With so much going on in the world, we can easily be distracted.

"Do you not know that those who run in a race all

run, but one receives the prize? Run in such a way that you may obtain it." — 1 Corinthians 9:24 (NKJV)

You can't win a race looking back. Spiritually speaking, all who run for Christ win the crown, but you can't allow your focus to be broken. When Jesus called Peter out to the deep waters, he was doing good until he focused on the storm. When he allowed his focus on Christ to be broken, he started sinking.

"Wherefore seeing we also are compassed about with so great a cloud of witnesses, let us lay aside every weight, and the sin which doth so easily beset us, and let us run with patience the race that is set before us." — Hebrews 12:1 (KJV)

When we allow our focus to be broken, we will start feeling defeated and crushed in spirit. We have to keep going. Man says there is no God. God says you're a fool if you don't believe I exist. What does the Bible say? God's Word is truth and what He says is already validated in Heaven. God's signature is in the creation. Who's right, God or man? Of course, God is always right.

"For the invisible things of him from the creation of the world are clearly seen, being understood by the things that are made, even his eternal power and Godhead; so that they are without excuse." —
Romans 1:20

The fool has said in his heart that there is no God. You can be sitting in church listening to the Word of God and be distracted by your cell phone, text, or messages when we should actually turn them off or put them on silent. Many false prophets have gone into the world, deceiving many, and they themselves are being deceived by Satan. Many have changed the truth of God into a lie and worshiped and served the creation more than the creator who is blessed forever. We see it today. Stay focused, or you will find yourself on the opposite team. They make the lie sound like the truth.

"No man can serve two masters: for either he will hate the one, and love the other; or else he will hold to the one, and despise the other. Ye cannot serve God and mammon." — Matthew 6:24

I saw a minister with a T-shirt on that said, "Hood N-Holy" Once you are saved, the hood part of you should no longer be a part of who you are. There should be something new about you from the inside out.

> "Therefore if any man be in Christ, he is a new creature: old things are passed away; behold, all things are become new." — 2 Corinthians 5:17 (KJV)

> "According as he hath chosen us in him before the foundation of the world, that we should be holy and without blame before him in love. — Ephesians 1:4 (KJV)

> "In Him you also trusted, after you heard the word of truth, the gospel of your salvation; in whom also, having believed, you were sealed with the Holy Spirit of promise." — Ephesians 1:13 (NKJV)

We were sealed with the Holy Spirit of promise. The Bible talks about how some are tossed to and fro and carried about with every wind of doctrine. Some people believe anything and everything. There will be things that will try to change the course of your life. If you get off track, you won't be able to reach your destination, Heaven. We're all on a path. Make sure you are on the path of Heaven.

"Commit your works to the Lord, and your thoughts will be established." — Proverbs 16:3

Listen up! Church attendance without salvation won't get you to Heaven stay focused on your eternal path.

"But the one who endures to the end will be saved." — Matthew 24:13 (NLT)

Steer clear of those who teach things that contradict what the Bible teaches. I call it another gospel, a gospel that doesn't line up with the Gospel of Jesus Christ. We've all messed up, and the only one that can turn your life around is Jesus Christ. I'm a witness.

"For we ourselves also were sometimes foolish, disobedient, deceived, serving divers lusts and pleasures, living in malice and envy, hateful, and hating one another." — Titus 3:3

"Foolish" refers to a lack of understanding of spiritual things. We were disobedient to God's Word. We were deceived into serving diverse lusts and pleasures, living in malice and envy, hateful and hating one another ... But God! When I got saved, I got redirected and refocused on the things of God. When you're focused, you know there aren't four or five ways to Heaven. Any other way is false. Jesus is the only way in.

> *"1 Verily, verily, I say unto you, He that entereth not by the door into the sheepfold, but climbeth up some other way, the same is a thief and a robber. 2 But he that entereth in by the door is the shepherd of the sheep. 3 To him the porter openeth; and the sheep hear his voice: and he calleth his own sheep by name, and leadeth them out." — John 10:1 (KJV)*

There are many voices out there trying to persuade you to listen to their voices. Jesus said in John 10:4, *"my sheep know my voice and a stranger they will not follow."* There are a lot of ministers who are preaching the true Word of God. Follow them. As you read the Word of God, you'll find that Jesus was always focused on His mission and assignment. He didn't allow the things people were saying to slow him down or get Him off course. He stayed the course and endured until the end, until He went back to Heaven.

His mission was to do God's will. He paid little attention to their praises. He wasn't trying to be famous.

"15 But when Jesus knew it, he withdrew himself from thence: and great multitudes followed him, and he healed them all; 16 And charged them that they should not make him known:" — Matthew 12:15-16

He would not allow the fame of His miracles to hinder his purpose of offering up Himself as a sacrifice for sin which was His real mission.

I don't take any glory for anything. I just thank God for gifting me with the gifts He has put on the inside of me to do an assignment in the earth. I want people to experience God through my music and ministry. I want to usher them into His presence, into His anointing. I know I have a purpose and a calling on my life.

Many people miss their true calling because they get so caught up in chasing the dollar. God appears to be nowhere in their sight because they are consumed with getting rich. I know this because I was once like that. Many were blessed to get rich but didn't know how to act when the money came. Riches do not make a fool cease from his foolishness. Even though he is rich, he is still a fool (Proverbs 14:24).

Perilous Times

2nd Timothy 3:1 gives us a preview of what the last days will be like. Watching the behaviors of mankind in these perilous times, it's like Satan has taken the minds and attitudes of many. It seems as if many people do not have a conscience to do right or to love one another. It reminds me of what Genesis 6:5 says, *"And God saw that the wickedness of man was great in the earth, and that every imagination of the thoughts of his heart was only evil continually."*

All these mass shootings, so many rappers getting gunned down over stupid stuff, COVID-19, and other pandemic crises affecting the whole world. Much of what we see on social media is insane, with many openly smoking blunt marijuana cigarettes online and many entertainers willingly or unwillingly admitting to having sold their souls to the devil. Jesus told us in His Word that right before He comes back, the world would be just like the days of Noah. He said that there would be famines, pestilence, and earthquakes in diverse places.

1st John 4:1 tells us not to believe every spirit, but to test the spirits to see whether they are of God. The criteria question is: is it biblical? The Bible also says that in these perilous times, iniquity shall abound and the love of many shall wax cold. In other words, those who once loved you suddenly change their minds about you for no reason at all.

Many people will betray and hate one another. People will hate you and become jealous of you for no reason at all. That includes family, friends, and church members. Many false prophets will arise and deceive many people. According to the Bible, all of these are the beginning of sorrows. Things are going to get worse. That's why we have to be alert and watchful.

Matthew 24:13-14 says, *"13 But he that shall endure unto the end, the same shall be saved. 14 And this gospel of the kingdom shall be preached in all the world for a witness unto all nations; and then shall the end come."* I believe it is nearer than we think.

"Watch therefore: for ye know not what hour your Lord doth come." — Matthew 24:42

Many today are not looking for Christ. They are living their lives like He is not coming back. Then, suddenly, He will appear. So much is going on in these perilous times. Hackers and scammers alike are trying to steal your money and information. Pimps in the pulpit who only care about how much money you can give them. The spirit of racism is on the rise.

Sometimes when I watch the news, it seems like the 1960s all over again. Hatred, suicide, depression, and just plain old foolishness are rampant in the young and old. There are problems in the government, problems with law enforcement. Look at what took place in Washington, DC when a mob took over the capital. We have never seen anything like this before. There is no respect for the government, the president, the capital officers, or the lawmakers, etc. Society, in many cases, has gotten wild and crazy. Dangerous times are here playing out right before our very eyes.

Wars And Rumors of Wars

Not only are there military wars, but a spiritual war is going on every day between good and evil, between God and Satan. Black on black crime, whites against blacks, attacks on Asian people, etc. A war is taking place in the Heavenlies. Terror is everywhere. There are problems at the borders of the United States where you see little kids being dropped or lowered over the walls, then put out there to fend for themselves.

There is a crisis in the world. All the things that we are witnessing are just the beginning of sorrows. Misery loves company today. A man in his depressed mental health state of mind decides that if he's not happy, he's going to go out and try to destroy others by shooting up schools, job sites, etc. It's crazy! But it shouldn't be a surprise because, again, Jesus said that the last days would be just like the days of Noah. So many people are stuck on stupid. Everybody is in a hurry. So much disrespect, and many don't have any integrity at all anymore.

The Bible tells us to watch and pray (Matthew 26:41), which means give strict attention to, be cautious and active in the things of God. Only what we do for Christ will last. Everything else will fade away. Always try to discern the spirit of a person because some people can be toxic, harmful, or malicious. Choose your friends wisely. Everybody is not meant to be in your life for a lifetime. Some are only for a reason, a season or a few for a lifetime.

One generation comes, another goes. Think about it. One hundred years from now, everyone on the earth today will be gone. Our life is simply a vapor. We are here for a moment, then we're gone. Don't get so caught up in this life that you don't prepare for the next one. We have to want the truth to get the truth. We, the church, the body of Christ, preachers, and teachers alike, need to quit coming against one another. We need to stop tearing down each other's teachings and beliefs unless it violates the written word of God.

No one has all the answers. Only God does, so preachers focus all that energy on reaching the lost and rescuing souls. Stop debating and arguing about the Word of God. We are all on borrowed time. These days are evil. Jesus is coming. Of course, all of us will agree to disagree, but there's strength in oneness and togetherness. Let's get on one accord.

Securing Your Eternal Future

It is so important for all of us to secure our eternal future with Jesus Christ, who was God manifested in the flesh. Like I've always said, all of us are on a journey going somewhere. Our earthly life is a journey that we travel on earth, and then we are gone. It's up to us to determine where we will go after our earthly journey ends. The decision must be made while we are alive. After we die, it is simply too late; your future will have already been determined.

If you find yourself at the great white throne of judgment, then you've waited too late. Many are not looking for the return of Jesus Christ. Most of us feel the world is changing. It's obvious. As Jesus said, He's coming back like a thief in the night. Many people will be caught off guard and not prepared. It reminds me of the story of the ten virgins in (Matthew 25:1-13). Some were ready, some were not. Those who were not ready slumbered and slept, while the others were prepared with all in their lamps. You can be blind in your thinking and what you believe. In all your getting, we must get understanding, rightly dividing the Word of Truth. We have to renew our minds and direction in life according to the Word of Truth.

Which way are you going? The journey is serious. Millions of people are traveling on roads that lead to a dead end. There's no power to transform them because they reject the only One who can save their soul, Jesus Christ. It takes the power of God to redirect our lives and clean us up. You are going to spend eternity somewhere. There are only two options: Heaven or Hell. It is my job and assignment to do the work of an evangelist. Let's look at the job of an evangelist. An evangelist travels from one place to another, spreading the Gospel message, preaching the word of God, proclaiming and communicating the Gospel of Jesus Christ to the world.

"But if our gospel be hid, it is hid to them that are lost." — 2 Corinthians 4:3

"For the preaching of the cross is to them that perish foolishness; but unto us which are saved it is the power of God." — 1 Corinthians 1:18

If you are not saved, you are lost. We must not allow anything to keep us from reaching Heaven when our time on earth is up. We must be in pursuit of Jesus because on that day, nothing else matters. We must be ready at all times, in ready mode to meet the King of Kings. Scripture says the Gospel is hid to those who are unsaved. It's like trying to see or read the Word of God with dirt in your eyes. You can't do it.

"Satan, who is the god of this world, has blinded the minds of those who don't believe. They are unable to see the glorious light of the Good News. They don't understand this message about the glory of Christ, who is the exact likeness of God." — 2 Corinthians 4:4

Satan attacks the central control system of your mind. We have to guard our minds, our hearts, our eyes and our ears. These are the gateways to our souls. Time is short. Jesus tells us to be alert. The enemy will try to darken your understanding. Satan likes to blind your mind with ignorance of God's Word. If we are in His Word daily, studying it to show ourselves approved unto God, Satan will not be able to trip you up with mess, with false doctrine, with things that are not biblical. There is the Spirit of Truth and the spirit of error. If what you believe doesn't point you to Jesus Christ, you need to go back and read.

> *"You search the Scriptures because you think they give you eternal life. But the Scriptures point to me!"* — *John 5:39*

> *"... if they speak not according to this word* (the Bible), *it is because there is no light in them."* — *Isaiah 8:20*

In this Scripture, the Lord God is saying, "If their message is different from mine, it is because I have not sent them. They have no light or truth in them." Romans 14:15 says, *"Let every man be fully persuaded in his own mind."* I was talking to a lady one day who was complaining about God and why He allowed people to starve and suffer. We were going back and forth about the Bible, so I said to her, "I hope when I get to Heaven, I see you there." She said to me, "Oh, you will, but not by way of Jesus." Wow! How wrong she was. The Bible says in Acts 4:12, *"Neither is there salvation in any other: for there is none other name under Heaven given among men, whereby we must be saved."* Jesus is also said that He is the way, the truth, and the life. He is the way into Heaven. No exceptions! It would be a shame to go to church all your life and at the end of your life you find out you weren't saved.

The Bible talks about how in the last days many will depart from the faith, giving heed to seducing spirits and doctrines of devils (1 Timothy 4:1). The door to eternal life is wide open. Jesus is standing at the door and knocking. Open up your heart and let Him in. It is one of the most important decisions that you will ever make. It is God's mercy that delays His judgment. Many wait until it's too late. Do it now. Do it in a hurry! Jesus is waiting to give more people the opportunity to repent and secure their eternal future. Say yes today, tomorrow is not promised.

The Bible tells us that Jesus is patient with us because He does not want anyone to perish. He wants everyone to come to repentance (2 Peter 3:3–

9). Many people would rather enjoy themselves now and not be concerned about the consequences they face later. A few minutes of pleasure is not worth spending eternity in Hell. Open your heart and examine your life. Ask yourself: Am I ready to meet God? Obeying God's rules is not up for debate, it is a command. It's up to you if you plan on spending eternity in Heaven with Him. So make the right choice.

We've all broken the rules; we've all fallen short. It's not about how you start, but how you finish. The Bible is the most controversial, the most hated, and the most loved book ever printed. It is also the best-selling book of all time, and its author is God. How can anyone hate and refuse something that gives us life? On judgment day, many will be without excuse.

Acts 4:12 says *"Neither is there salvation in any other"* (but Jesus). We are living in very perilous times. We need the Lord's protection in a world full of darkness. We have to search the Scriptures because they point to Jesus (John 5:39). The Bible is the only book in the world that gives us all a preview of the future.

"All Scripture is inspired by God and is useful to teach us what is true and to make us realize what is wrong in our lives. It corrects us when we are wrong and teaches us to do what is right." — 2 Timothy 3:16

Dead Man Walking

Those who are not saved are spiritually dead, walking around in the earth. They are just existing. We, as born-again Christians, need to be evangelizing. We cannot be so busy having church among ourselves while the world is going to Hell. We have to get out among the dead and wake them up with the Gospel of Jesus Christ. There is a TV show called *"The Walking Dead."* Hollywood comes up with mess like this, but that's not reality. The dead don't walk around. What is dead is dead. Most don't realize there is a spirit world that we go to after we die, and people are not walking around like the TV show displays. After the saved die here on earth, they enter Heaven where they will walk around worshiping and praising God. But for the unsaved, it's another story. The unsaved will be in Hell and torment day and night, and believe me, they will not be walking around.

Isaiah 5:14 says *"Hell hath enlarged herself and opened her mouth without measure."* Which means

Hell can receive more and more souls and never get full and overflow. It can hold every person who chooses to go there. Jesus says in 2 Peter 3:9 that He is not willing (does not want) that any should perish but that all should come to repentance. Deuteronomy 30:19 says, *"I call Heaven and earth as witnesses today against you, that I have set before you life and death, blessing and cursing; therefore choose life, that both you and your descendants may live."*

Many of us have heard about pandemics in the past, never thinking we would experience one in our lifetime. In 1918, the world experienced the Spanish Flu, which reportedly killed 20 to 50 million people. As COVID-19 caught all of us by surprise, so will the rapture. The second coming of Christ will catch billions off guard. We're living in a time where we must get serious about our spiritual life and our eternal future. Many people are dead to the things of God. All of us, at one time or another, walked in darkness according to the course of this world (before salvation) with no savior insight. But thank God we came out of that lifestyle to pursue what's more important, the things of God. "

Proverbs 3:7 says, *"Be not wise in thine own eyes: fear the Lord and depart from evil."* There are so many people today who are greedy for gain. They will do anything to get ahead, even at another's expense. It becomes all about them. Whether the world is in a crisis or not, the behavior of the wicked will continue in spite of the conditions. To be spiritually dead is to be separated from God. There are no free passes into Heaven. Only born-again Believers will enter Heaven. If you're not a born-again Believer (a Christian), you're a dead man walking.

We must remember that Satan is that spirit at work in the hearts of those who refuse to obey God and get saved. The Lord Jesus wants to give us an awesome life with Him beyond this life, if we choose to accept it. Many people have sold their souls to the devil in exchange for fame and fortune. In Revelation 21:18, the Word of God gives us a foretaste of what the future will be like with the Lord, as well as a glimpse of a future in Hell if you reject Christ. Don't walk the earth in a dead spiritual condition. Accept Jesus Christ as your Lord and Savior and come alive to the things of God.

Are you ready to meet Him? We have got to have a made-up mind to serve Him or be lost. Where do you plan on spending eternity? Many today are playing Russian Roulette with their souls. Many do not even realize that they are on the brink of a major decision that could alter their life forever. Let every man examine their own self.

In John 11:25 Jesus said, *"I am the resurrection and the life. He who believes in Me, though he may die* (physically), *he shall live."* If you don't have Jesus, you're not going to experience Heaven. Satan wants to stop every true ministry that's spreading the Gospel of Jesus Christ, and he doesn't care who he uses to do it. We are on his hit list, but you can't stop what God has ordained. At the moment of death, the Believer is ushered into the presence of God. Many people die without any hope beyond the grave because they refuse to prepare for eternity while they are alive. Don't let it be you.

Hell is real. When the rich man in the book of

Luke went to Hell, he knew he was doomed there forever and ever. He cried out and said, "Father Abraham, have mercy on me, and send Lazarus, that he may dip the tip of his finger in water, and cool my tongue; for I am tormented in this flame." Abraham said, "There is a great chasm separating us. No one can cross over to you from here, and no one can cross over to us from there."

The rich man said, "I beg you, send Lazarus to my father's house, for I have five brothers, that he may testify to them, lest they also come to this place of torment." Abraham said to him, "They have Moses and the prophets; let them hear them." The rich man said, "No, Father Abraham! But if someone is sent to them from the dead, then they will repent of their sins and turn to God." Abraham said, "If they do not hear Moses and the prophets, neither will they be persuaded though one rises from the dead."

The rich man's money couldn't buy him anything in the spirit realm. It carried no weight. His prayers were unheard; they couldn't help him. It was too late to warn anyone that he loved and cared about on earth. His money couldn't buy him a measure of relief.

> *"13 But I would not have you to be ignorant, brethren, concerning them which are asleep, that ye sorrow not, even as others which have no hope. 14 For if we believe that Jesus died and rose again, even so them also which sleep in Jesus will God bring with him." —1 Thessalonians 4:13-14*

> *"And many of them that sleep in the dust of the earth shall awake, some to everlasting life, and some to shame and everlasting contempt." — Daniel 12:2*

Why? Because the unsaved reject Christ during their lifetime and fail to live by His standards. When we leave this life, we will instantly and supernaturally travel from earth to the 3rd Heaven, where God is. We will travel to another dimension, leaving this old life behind. When we all get to Heaven, what a time that will be. When we give our life to the Lord, we have great things to look forward to. If you reject Him, you have nothing but eternal darkness and torment in Hell where you will be forever and ever.

The Rapture will supernaturally transport Believers who are alive into the clouds where Jesus will be.

We'll meet Him in the air, and we'll be with Him forever. If a Believer in Christ dies before the rapture takes place, angels will be assigned to transport you into the presence of God. What a day to look forward to. We are living in a stubborn and evil generation, and God is not going to rewrite the Bible for our generation. The Word of God is final. It's a blueprint for us to live by. Actually, the Lord has given all of us another day to start over. We have to reset our lives and follow Jesus and keep pressing toward the mark for the high calling.

Hell Is a Real Place

I want to talk about a subject that most ministers don't talk about much anymore. You or someone you know may be in serious spiritual danger. This chapter is not to scare you but to warn or alert you about what lies beyond the grave if you haven't accepted Jesus Christ as Lord and savior. Many, not a few, will come to Him, saying, "Lord, Lord," and His response will be, "Depart from me." I never knew you, which means you are a stranger to Him.

People will say to you, even the drunks, even the drug dealers, etc., "Well, I love the Lord, but Jesus said if you love me, you'll do what I say." Many will say, "Oh, I know the Lord, but does he know you? Will the demon say to you, as in Acts 19:15, "Jesus I know, Paul I know, but who are you?" If I thought I could scare you into Heaven to avoid Hell, I would. Millions of people hear heartfelt messages every day. Most don't let it faze them, and they go right on doing whatever they want to do.

A lot of people make a good start, but many fall by the wayside and give up. We are all in a spiritual war and the end result could be good or bad. It depends on the choice you make. Many people (1,000,000) have already gone to Hell, and millions more will join them. Only the Lord Jesus Christ can save you from this awful place of torment. We must keep in mind that this life will end one day. We could die suddenly without any warning! And none of us can hold back our spirits from departing (Ecclesiastes 8:8). None of us has the power to prevent the day of our death. Then what?

Death is not going to come up to you and say, "You know you are getting ready to die, don't you?" No, it happens when we least expect it. If you fail to choose to serve God, you have chosen to serve the devil. Many refuse to accept that God would send anyone to Hell or that a place like this even exists, but Jesus talked about Heaven and Hell, so who are you going to believe? Satan's greatest weapon is deception. There are no second chances in eternity. The choice is yours to make. If you haven't received Jesus Christ as Lord and Savior, do it in a hurry!

It's truly about reaching souls. Millions are rushing into Hell. Proverbs 11:30 tells us, "The fruit of the righteous is a tree of life, and he who wins souls is wise." When we tell others about Christ, we are presenting to them a tree of life. We are mandated as born-again believers to reach the lost. God needs laborers to harvest and those that are on their way to Hell.

> *"Repent therefore and be converted, that your sins may be blotted out, so that times of refreshing may come from the presence of the Lord," —* Acts 3:19 (NKJV)

It is about being transformed. Only the power of God can do that. I was talking to a man one day, and he said to me, "I want to just drink myself to death and just leave the earth without feeling it." What this man didn't realize is that if he leaves this world in a drunken state without Jesus, he would feel the pain and torment in Hell. Many teach and believe that death is the end of everything. After death, you don't exist anymore. Physically on earth, you don't exist anymore, but the moment you die, your spirit and soul are going to exit your body into eternity somewhere.

Reading the story of Lazarus and the rich man in Luke in Chapter 16, you will notice that the man was very much alive after death, and he felt everything that was happening in Hell. This passage of Scripture talks about two people, one rich and one poor, who died. One died and was buried and was carried by the angels to Abraham's Bosom. The other died and was buried and was in torment. Here we see two people with different outcomes when they died. It depends on the choice you made while you were alive. After you die, it is too late.

"For what will it profit a man if he gains the whole world, and loses his own soul?" — Mark 8:36 NKJV

There is life after death, whether you believe it or not. Everyone that dies in Christ goes to Heaven. Everyone who dies without Christ goes to Hell. You don't have to question what I say. Read the Bible for yourself. Jesus is knocking at the door of your heart. Don't snooze, don't reject God's offer of salvation. Today, if you hear his voice, do not harden your hearts. Don't snooze when He's knocking on the door. Don't delay your response. Seek Him while He can be found.

We don't have time to waste. Avoid Hell. Make Jesus a part of your everyday life. Jesus is trying to keep many out of Hell by knocking at the door of their hearts, but they answer with "I'm not ready to be saved" or "Who's there?" or "Can you come back tomorrow?" or they don't answer at all. Something happens when God fills us with His Spirit and begins to transform us (*see Revelation 3:20*). Don't make the mistake of dying without Jesus. Your soul is at stake. Hell is a real place. Jesus said so.

Sodom of Today

The Bible talks about Sodom and Gomorrah of yesterday. Today is no different. There's nothing new under the sun. Jesus said in the last days the world would be just like in the days of Noah and Sodom and Gomorrah. The destruction of Sodom and Gomorrah was based on a real-life event. Many today are rude, evil, and have hearts that have waxed cold. The manifestations of what went on in that city is repeating itself in cities all across the world. Men with men, women with women openly kissing and hugging right on our television and in the movies and commercials, and it is accepted as normal. Ecclesiastes 1:4 says, *"One generation passes away, and another generation comes, but the earth abides forever."*

We're living in a dangerous hour now with these wars and rumors of wars going on. The old Sodom and Gomorrah passed away, and now we're living in the Sodom of today, where wickedness is stronger than in the former place. There is some good in social media to get biblical information out, but 90% of it is wicked, with so much lewdness and indecent behavior shown right on social media. What a shame! Violent crime is everywhere. So many women are putting themselves on display like harlots (prostitutes). Statistics say a murder occurs every 25 minutes, a forceable rape every 10 minutes, a robbery every 60 seconds, and an aggravated assault occurs every 55 seconds. The inmate population has grown to over 2 million-plus and is steadily growing. With so much going on, it has caused a paralyzing fear in society. As Jesus said, people are living only to satisfy their appetites and material desires, doing everything they can imagine. you have to look over your shoulders everywhere you go.

Genesis 6:5 says The Lord observed the extent of human wickedness on the earth, and he saw that everything they thought or imagined was consistently and totally evil. And it has continued since that time to this time and God even sees today that the wickedness of man is great in the earth.

Wickedness In the Earth

Trouble is everywhere in the home, in the streets,

in the schools, in the mall, in the church, on the job etc. Bible history tells us the story of the flood when evil was rampant in the earth because the hearts of man were only on evil continually. We're living now on borrowed time. These days are evil. We all must prepare for the coming of the Lord. Tragic things are happening so suddenly and unexpectedly that no human can predict what tomorrow will bring. Only God knows. Use caution in who you listen to and who you choose to take guidance from. Satan's goal is to make you quit. We must be concerned about our purpose and about God's will. What's taking up your time? What is the value of your soul? God has given all of us 24 hours in a day. There are 1400 minutes in a day, 168 hours in a week, and 365 days in a year.

> "15 So be careful how you live. Don't live like fools, but like those who are wise. 16 Make the most of every opportunity in these evil days. 17 Don't act thoughtlessly but understand what the Lord wants you to do." —Ephesians 5:15-17 NLT

The world is spinning out of control people everywhere beginning to live in a state of fear our time is brief on earth compared to eternity.

"All of us, like sheep, have strayed away. We have left God's paths to follow our own. Yet the Lord laid on him the sins of us all. — Isaiah 53:6

We must make a U-turn and repent let God use you in these last days the path of eternal life is through Jesus Christ. we must fulfill God's agenda while there is still time.

In Psalm 90:12, the psalmist prays, *"Teach us to number our days, that we may apply our hearts unto wisdom."* God is not slack concerning His return. We just have to be ready. God has assigned to each of us a birthdate and a death date. It is appointed unto man once to die, but after that comes judgment (Hebrews 9:27). God has assigned to us a certain number of days, and they are quickly ticking away. God has a specific purpose for our lives. He said, "I know the plans I have for you." But we try to make our own plans and miss out on the real purpose for our life on earth. How much time do we have on earth? Nobody knows. It can happen suddenly without any warning. Then we are gone.

Over the course of months since COVID-19 hit

the world, thousands of people have died. Many have been pressed or troubled in every way, losing jobs, loved ones, income, having no food, etc. and the powers to be (government) struggling because they don't know what to do, leaving them powerless over the unseen evil virus. This virus is in the air, so who is the prince of the power of the air? It is Satan. The world is in a crisis. Hospitals can't even accommodate the massive overflow of people. God help us.

We are pressed (troubled) on every side by troubles, but not crushed and broken. We are perplexed, but we are haunted down but God never abandons us we get knocked down, but we get up again keep going (2 Corinthians 4:8). I'm in it to win it I'm going all the way to the finish line short days to make choices that will bring eternal consequences.

The Heart Of A Soldier

A soldier is a person who serves the heart of a soldier in an army, one that is engaged in military service. It's about being an effective warrior and proclaiming the Gospel of Jesus Christ to the world. A soldier in the Kingdom of God is someone who is trained for physical and spiritual warfare between good and evil. In this fight, our enemy is a spirit being named Satan. God wants us to be spiritually on guard.

"10 Finally, my brethren, be strong in the Lord and in the power of His might. 11 Put on the whole armor of God, that you may be able to stand against the wiles of the devil. 12 For we do not wrestle against flesh and blood, but against principalities, against powers, against the rulers of the darkness of this age, against spiritual hosts of wickedness in the Heavenly places." — Ephesians 6:10-12 NKJV

God has equipped us with the necessary tools to fight this enemy of our soul. The branch that we have been drafted into is God's Army, but you must be born again. Jesus said, *"If you are not with me, you are against me."* I've never been in the military, but at the age of 26, I became a soldier, not for the United States, but for the Kingdom of God. I was called, appointed, and anointed by God to serve Him and to complete an assignment He has given me.

> *"3 You therefore must endure hardship as a good soldier of Jesus Christ. 4 No one engaged in warfare entangles himself with the affairs of this life, that he may please him who enlisted him as a soldier." — 2 Timothy 2:3-4*

A soldier has one thing on his mind, and that is to carry out his duty as a soldier using his training so that he may please him who chose him to be a soldier. Satan targeted the human race in his war against God and all who worship God. Satan hates us. He carries out his warfare through a well-organized army of evil spirits. One thing about being a soldier is that you can't be afraid to fight. We've got to fight for our souls. A true soldier of the Lord will defend the Gospel. He'll speak what God speaks. The Great Commission is a personnel directive from Jesus to all His followers.

A Money Driven Society

"The silver is Mine, and the gold is Mine,' says the Lord of hosts." — Haggai 2:8

The love of money sometimes leads to destruction, and it's the root of all evil. There is nothing wrong with having money, but don't let it have you to the point that you will do anything for it. The grip that money can have over one's life can push one to resort to doing all sorts of things just to get it. Many are losing their lives and their freedom by committing armed robbery, murder, scams, burglaries, prostitution, sex trafficking, etc., and a whole lot of trickery.

Most of the population of the world never thinks they have enough money. The search for money never ends. All of us want more. Most chase the dollar bill and never give much attention to the things of God and the Lord Jesus Christ. Money will not buy you a ticket into Heaven. Don't allow trying to get money to cause you to miss Heaven.

About The Author

Robert was born to parents Robert & Barbara Scott he was the first of six children born in Atlanta, Georgia. He started singing at an early age (12) and had his dreams of being a Recording Artist, he came from a family of Journalists. His family started the nation's first black-owned newspaper "The Atlanta Daily World" which his great-uncle W. A. Scott, II was the founder. Robert was not interested in journalism but had a love for music. So that's what he pursued. Writing would find a place in his heart later in life with the self-publishing of two books: "Reflections of My Life (2008)" and "Which Way Are You Going?" (2013).

His music has been heard on Atlanta Gospel stations Love 86, WCLK, WAOK, WYZE, WBAH in Cartersville, Georgia and Internet Radio & Internet T.V. including appearing on "The Reggie Gay Gospel Show

With Singer Nat George and A Time In The Word With Sarah Hurd. Robert's Gospel Journey has allowed him to appear in many churches from Georgia to Florida. This anointed singer has one thing in mind, reaching souls for The Kingdom of God and being about God's business.

Today, Robert balances home life and his ministry of music & writing for the purpose of reaching hearts for the Lord.

To book Robert for an event e-mail him at:

- bayrob56@gmail.com

Other Books available on Amazon.com:

- Reflections Of My Life
- Which Way Are You Going

YouTube Videos

- I'm Glad (I'm Saved)
- Kingdom Business
- Thirsty
- Your Faith ft. Dereck McCuller
- Heaven
- Atlanta Live Interview